MENDELSSOHN
Six Christmas Pieces
Opus 72

Willard A. Palmer, *Editor*
Based on the original edition.

Mendelssohn at the age of twenty-two, painted in Rome by Horace Vernet, 1831.

Contents

If the title "Six Christmas Pieces" for Mendelssohn's Opus 72 is a surprise to some, it must be explained that this is exactly the English title that Mendelssohn himself designated for this work. The title is an appropriate one, since it reflects the fresh, ebullient, happy and simple charm of these miniatures. Like Schumann's "Scenes from Childhood," they might well have been intended to reflect the joys associated with the experiences of the very young as seen through the eyes of older people. They are in no sense Kindergarten works. They are valuable material for young pianists and for older students. In form they may be regarded as "Songs Without Words." Their value as teaching material is unmistakable. They contain a wealth of musical challenge and their musical messages are invariably interesting and clear.

Opus 72 was completed during a visit to England in 1842, and is the next work Mendelssohn composed after completing his Scotch Symphony.

Six Christmas Pieces

I

Allegro non troppo ♩=104

Felix Mendelssohn, Op. 72

3

III

Allegretto ♩=76

IV

Andante con moto ♩.=60

9

V

VI